BIBLE BOOT CAMP:

HOW TO STUDY THE BIBLE

VOLUME 2

C. MICHAEL PATTON

TIMOHTY G. KIMBERLEY

CREDO HOUSE

ISBN-13: 978-1456453152

ISBN-10: 1456453157

Printed in the United States of America

www.credohouse.org

CONTENTS

BASIC TRAINING:THE PROCESS

THE INTERPRETIVE PROCESS

Bridging the Historical Gap

Bridging the Literary Gap

Bridging the Contextual Gap

SOME COMMON BIBLE STUDY METHODS:

Lucky lotto: (eyes closed) – "I will read this verse"

Brussels Sprout: "Do I have to?"

Channel Changer: "Let's read something else"

Concord: "Watch how fast I can finish"

Baseball card: "I'm very picky"

Clint Eastwood: "I don't need anyone's help"

Magical: "Abracadabra . . . It applies to my life"

Indiana Jones: "Let's find the hidden meaning"

BASIC TRAINING: THE PROCESS

Interpretation: The process by which the Scriptures are understood by the reader.

Hermeneutics: The theory, method, or rules of biblical interpretation.

Exegesis: Gk. ex, "out" + hegeisthai, "to lead." The process of discovering the original meaning of the biblical text by studying the text according to the authorial intent in its historical contexts.

TIMELESS AUDIENCE

2. WHAT DOES IT MEAN?

 TIME BOUND AUDIENCE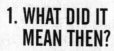

1. WHAT DID IT MEAN THEN?

ANCIENT AUDIENCE

3. HOW DOES IT APPLY TODAY?

CONTEMPORARY AUDIENCE

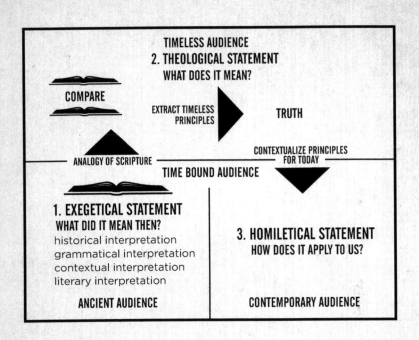

TIMELESS AUDIENCE
2. THEOLOGICAL STATEMENT
WHAT DOES IT MEAN?

COMPARE

EXTRACT TIMELESS PRINCIPLES

TRUTH

ANALOGY OF SCRIPTURE

CONTEXTUALIZE PRINCIPLES FOR TODAY

TIME BOUND AUDIENCE

1. EXEGETICAL STATEMENT
WHAT DID IT MEAN THEN?
historical interpretation
grammatical interpretation
contextual interpretation
literary interpretation

ANCIENT AUDIENCE

3. HOMILETICAL STATEMENT
HOW DOES IT APPLY TO US?

CONTEMPORARY AUDIENCE

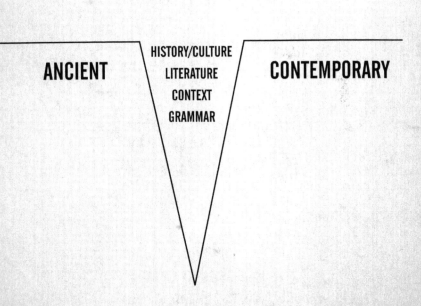

ANCIENT

HISTORY/CULTURE
LITERATURE
CONTEXT
GRAMMAR

CONTEMPORARY

 # COMBAT TRAINING:PROCESS

THEOLOGICAL EISEGESIS FALLACY:

Gk. eis, "in" + hegeisthai, "to lead."

The process of conforming the text to your presupposed system of belief.

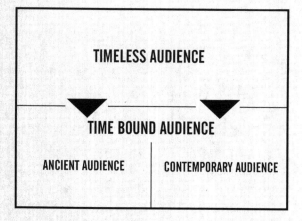

ARCHAIC APPLICATION FALLACY:

The process of directly applying Scripture without extracting the timeless principles.

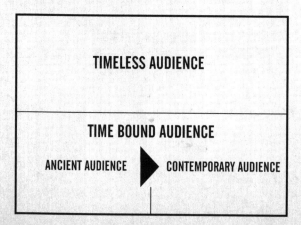

FIELD MANUAL:PROCESS

2 TIMOTHY 2:15

"Be diligent to present yourself approved to God as a workman who does not need to be ashamed, handling accurately the word of truth."

JOSH. 1:8

"This book of the law shall not depart from your mouth, but you shall meditate on it day and night, so that you may be careful to do according to all that is written in it; for then you will make your way prosperous, and then you will have success."

FIRST COMMANDMENT

EX. 20:1–3

1 And God spoke all these words:
2 "I am the Lord your God, who brought you out of Egypt, out of the land of slavery.
3 "You shall have no other gods before me.

DEUT. 5:7
ISA. 44:8
JER. 25:6
1 TIM. 2:5

TIMELESS AUDIENCE
2. THEOLOGICAL STATEMENT
God warns people not to have misguided hope in anything that could displace Him as their true source of trust, but to rest ultimately in Him for all things.

ANALOGY OF SCRIPTURE

CONTEXTUALIZE PRINCIPLES FOR TODAY

TIME BOUND AUDIENCE

1. EXEGETICAL STATEMENT
God warned the Isrealites, who had just agreed to become His covenanted people, who just left a polytheistic culture that trusted in their gods for provisions, not to place trust in any other gods, but to place all their trust in Him.

ANCIENT AUDIENCE

3. HOMILETICAL STATEMENT
Don't set your heart to the pursuit of the things that would replace God as the ultimate source of your trust. Rest only and completely on Him.

CONTEMPORARY AUDIENCE

FIELD OPS:PROCESS

ADDITIONAL TRAINING:

Living by the Book by Howard Hendricks

Basic Bible Interpretation by Roy Zuck

Introduction to Biblical Interpretation by Craig Blomberg
http://www.reclaimingthemind.org/blog/2010/04/bible-interpretation-in-a-nutshell/

GROUP DISCUSSION QUESTIONS:

1. Under the "Some Common Bible Study Methods" section, which one do you find most in the church today? Explain.

2. Let's get personal: Under the "Some Common Bible Study Methods" section, which one do you find most in your life today? Explain.

3. What is the biggest fear you have about "exegeting" the Scripture? Explain

4. Give one or two examples about how you have seen either the Theological Fallacy or the Archaic Application Fallacy practiced.

2. BRIDGING THE HISTORICAL GAP

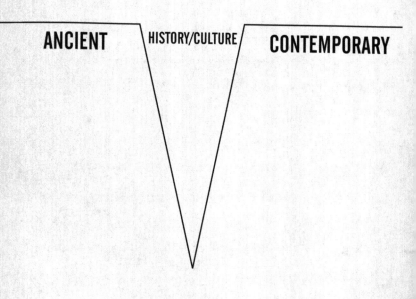

ANCIENT   HISTORY/CULTURE   CONTEMPORARY

BASIC TRAINING:HISTORICAL GAP

Most of the Bible is more than two-thousand years old. There is a historical/cultural gap that must be bridged.

HISTORICAL ISSUES TO CONSIDER:

Author: Who wrote the book?

Date: When was it written?

Audience: Who was it written to?

Circumstances/Purpose(s): What was going on at the time? Why was it written?

TWO AVENUES FOR HISTORICAL RESEARCH:

Internal Data – What can we learn from the text itself?

External Data – What extra-biblical historical evidence is available to us?

EXTERNAL DATA:

Archaeology

Bible commentaries

Secondary background research

Primary background research

"CULTURE SHOCK"

When you go to live in a different country, what are some of the customs that you need to be aware of?

What are some of the customs that we have that are unique to our culture?

"When a missionary goes to a foreign land, he must know what the people in that culture think, believe, say, do, and make. He must understand their culture in order to comprehend them and thus communicate properly with them. If you have traveled to a foreign country, you have no doubt experienced some degree of 'culture shock.' This means you were jolted by the unfamiliar scenes and practices of the people in that nation. . . . When we go to the Scriptures, it is as if we are entering a foreign land."

– Roy Zuck

POLITICAL

ECONOMIC

AGRICULTURAL

FAMILY

ARCHITECTURAL

SOCIAL

RELIGIOUS

GEOGRAPHICAL

LEGAL

MILITARY

DIETARY

CLOTHING

PHILOSOPHICAL CULTURE

COMBAT TRAINING:HISTORICAL GA

PRACTICAL EISEGESIS FALLACY:

Gk. eis, "in" + h geisthai, "to lead."

Also called "reader response"

The process of conforming the text to your current circumstance, making it more relevant and applicable.

TIMELESS AUDIENCE

TIME BOUND AUDIENCE

ANCIENT AUDIENCE   **CONTEMPORARY AUDIENCE**

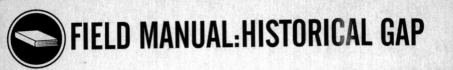

MATT. 8:21-22

"And another of the disciples said to Him, 'Lord, permit me first to go and bury my father.' But Jesus said to him, 'Follow Me; and allow the dead to bury their own dead.'"

REV. 3:14-16

"To the angel of the church in Laodicea write: The Amen, the faithful and true Witness, the Beginning of the creation of God, says this: 'I know your deeds, that you are neither cold nor hot; I wish that you were cold or hot. So because you are lukewarm, and neither hot nor cold, I will spit you out of My mouth.'"

PLAGUE	GOD REBUKED
NILE TO BLOOD	HAPI, GOD OF THE NILE
FROGS	HEQET, GODDESS WITH FROG HEAD
GNATS	SET, GOD OF DESERT
FLIES	UARCHIT, FLY IDOL
LIVESTOCK DEATH	APIS, BULL GOD
BOILS	ISIS, GODDESS OF HEALING
HAIL	SET, GOD OF STORMS
LOCUSTS	OSIRIS, GOD OF CROPS
DARKNESS	RE, SUN GOD
DEATH OF FIRSTBORN	ISIS, GODDESS PROTECTED CHILDREN

SECOND COMMANDMENT:
EX. 20:4-5

You shall not make for yourself a carved image or any likeness of anything that is in heaven or above, or that is on earth or under it, or that is in the water below. You shall not bow down to them or serve them.

2 CHRON.6:18
PS. 113:5
ISA. 66:1
1 TIM. 6:16

TIMELESS AUDIENCE
2. THEOLOGICAL STATEMENT
God warns believers not to misrepresent God's holy and transcendent nature in hopes of having more sight to our trust.

ANALOGY OF SCRIPTURE

CONTEXTUALIZE PRINCIPLES FOR TODAY

TIME BOUND AUDIENCE

1. EXEGETICAL STATEMENT
God tells the Isrealites that they are not to make a representation of Him that is made from creation so that they could trust in what they see, as did the Egyptians.

ANCIENT AUDIENCE

3. HOMILETICAL STATEMENT
Worship God as the holy and transcendent One that He is, resisting the temptation and need to see with your eyes Him whom no eye can see.

CONTEMPORARY AUDIENCE

FIELD OPS:HISTORICAL GAP

ADDITIONAL TRAINING:

The IVP Bible Background Commentary:
New Testament, Craig Keener

The IVP Bible Background Commentary:
Old Testament, John H. Walton

Manners and Customs of the Bible, J. I. Packer
Zondervan Illustrated Bible Backgrounds Commentary
Old & New Testaments, 9 Volumes, Clinton E. Arnold

GROUP DISCUSSION QUESTIONS:

1. Describe a time when you have experienced "culture shock."

2. Why do you think it is so common to ignore the history of the Bible?

3. Give one or two examples about how you have seen the Practical Eisegesis Fallacy practiced.

4. How did this lesson challenge you most?

3. BRIDGING THE LITERARY GAP

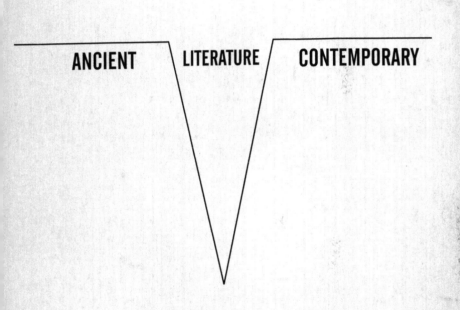

ANCIENT   LITERATURE   CONTEMPORARY

"There is a...sense in which the Bible, since it is after all literature, cannot be properly read except as literature; and the different parts of it as the different sorts of literature they are."

- C.S. Lewis

PROV. 22:6

"Train up a child in the way he should go, even when he is old he will not depart from it."

Genre: A category of literature which is to read and interpreted according to distinct and specific rules that are assumed upon the writing.

What types of genres do we have today?

EDITORIALS
FICTION
FACEBOOK STATUS
NON-FICTION HISTORIES
DICTIONARIES
EMAILS
TEXT MESSAGES
TWITTER UPDATES
LOVE LETTERS
BIOGRAPHIES
AUTOBIOGRAPHIES
HANDBOOKS FOR "DUMMIES"
INSTRUCTION MANUALS
CHILDREN'S BOOKS
TEXTBOOKS

Genesis, Exodus, Leviticus, Numbers, Deuteronomy, Joshua, Judges, Ruth, 1 Samuel, 2 Samuel, 1 Kings, 2 Kings, 1 Chronicles, 2 Chronicles, Ezra, Nehemiah, Esther	History/Narrative	To give a theological history of Isreal in narrative form
Psalms	Poetry	Emotional praises and cries to God
Job, Proverbs, Ecclesiastes, Song of Solomon	Wisdom	Instructions for wise living
Isaiah, Jeremiah, Lamentations, Ezekiel, Daniel, Hosea, Joel, Amos, Obadiah, Jonah, Micah, Nahum, Habakkuk, Zephaniah, Haggai, Zechariah, Malachi	Prophecy	Call Isreal to repentance
Matthew, Mark, Luke, John, Acts	History/Narrative	To give a theological history of Christ
Romans, 1 Corinthians, 2 Corinthians, Galatians, Ephesians, Philippians, Colossians, 1 Thessalonians, 2 Thessalonians, 1 Timothy, 2 TimothyTitus, Philemon, Hebrews, James, 1 John, 2 John, 3 John, Jude	Epistle	Didactic and Pastoral letters written to explain Theological teaching for the Church
Revelation	Apacolyptic	Message of hope for the Church

The Scriptures were not written in a "Bible" type of literature or an inspired genre. God accommodated his word into the language and literature of man.

TYPES LITERATURE (GENRES) IN THE BIBLE:

History/Narrative

Poetry

Wisdom

Prophecy

Epistle/Letter

Apocalyptic

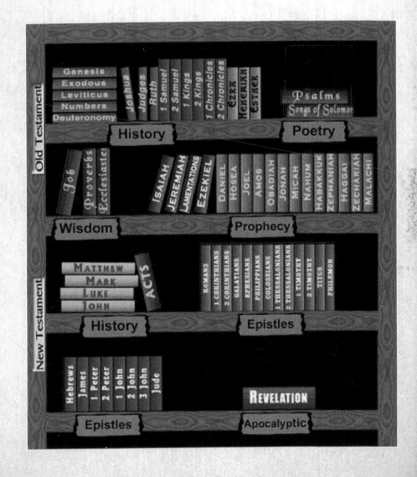

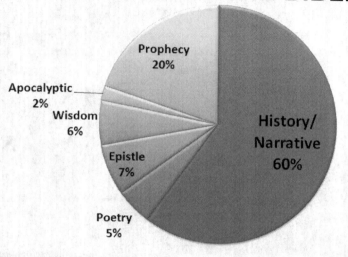

GENRES IN THE BIBLE

Prophecy 20%

Apocalyptic 2%

Wisdom 6%

Epistle 7%

Poetry 5%

History/ Narrative 60%

HISTORY/NARRATIVE

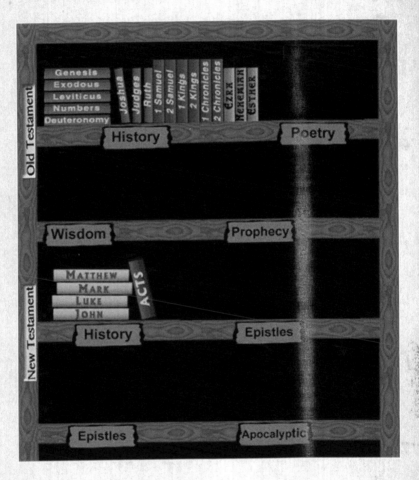

CHARACTERISTICS OF HISTORY/NARRATIVE:

Telling a story about which the parts cannot be isolated from the whole.

Character development

Plot, climax, resolution

Theological in nature

Easy to remember

"Biblical narratives tell us about things that happened— but not just any things. Their purpose is to show God at work in his creation and among his people. The narratives glorify him, help us to understand and appreciate him, and give us a picture of his providence and protection. At the same time they also provide illustrations of many other lessons important to our lives"

Gordon D. Fee and Douglas Stuart, How to Read the Bible for All Its Worth, 79

POETRY

Artistic writing birthed from the emotional disposition of the writer that served in prayer, worship, and praise to God.

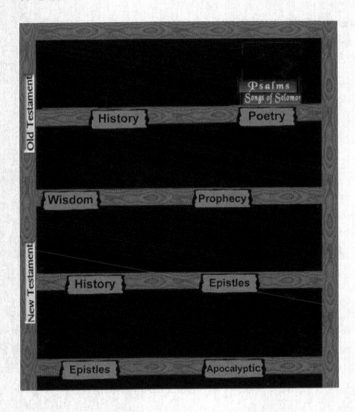

CHARACTERISTICS OF POETRY

Follows a rhythm

Easy to memorize

Often contains a prophetic element (Messianic Psalms)

Emotional

Parallelisms

Much symbolism

Calls for judgment (imprecatory)
Cries to God (laments)
Songs of praise
Basic Training
Lament Psalm

LAMENT PSALM
PSA. 13:1

"How long, O LORD? Will you forget me forever? How long will you hide your face from me?"

IMPRECATORY PSALM
PSA. 55:15

"Let death come deceitfully upon my enemies; Let them go down alive to the grave, for evil is in their dwelling, in their midst."

SYNONYMOUS PARALLEL PSALM:

The second line restates the thought of the first line using different words.

PSA. 2:4

He who sits in the heavens laughs,
The Lord scoffs at them.

WISDOM

Literature intended to teach about transcendent truth and values, giving keen insights into virtuous living.

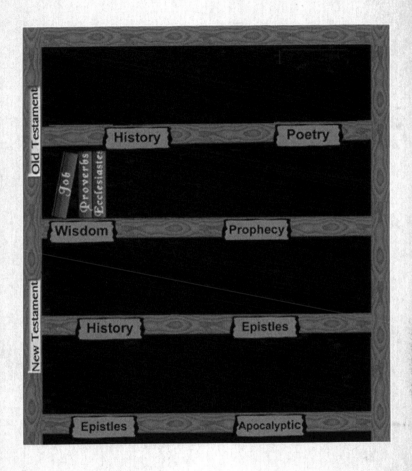

CHARACTERISTICS OF WISDOM:

Intended to produce a godly perspective and character.

Sometimes birthed in and through negative circumstances.

Normally already in principles.

General observable truths, not promises.

Often short and pithy with limited context.
Written to convert the naïve.

Easy to misunderstand, especially in Job and Eccl.

PROPHECY

Prophets were "covenant enforcement mediators" who spoke on behalf of God to Israel and the nations. Their writings served as announcements, calls to repentance, and warnings.

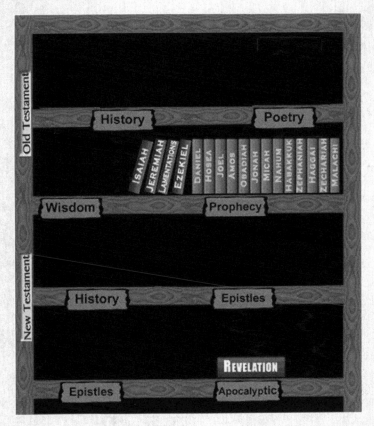

CHARACTERISTICS OF PROPHECY:

Closest thing in the Old Testament to an epistle.

The primary function of a prophet in the OT was "forth telling" – speaking to people for God.

Often direct announcement of God: "Thus says the Lord. . ."

Must discern whether the audience is theocratic Israel or all people.

Announcements of things both far and near
Often highly symbolic.

Apocalyptic prophecy deals only with the end of the world.

EPISTLE/LETTER

Epistles are letters written to an individual, group, or public audience. The main distinction between a letter and an epistle is that an epistle is a letter intended for the public in general.

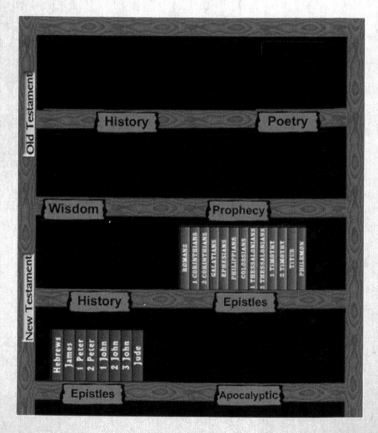

CHARACTERISTICS OF AN EPISTLE/LETTER

Greeting, body, farewell

Occasional letters often addressing one or more problems

Written in the church age to people in the church Logical flow: "for," "therefore," "just as"

COMBAT TRAINING:LITERARY GAP

INCIDENTAL FALLACY:
Reading incidental historical texts as prescriptive rather than descriptive.

PRESCRIPTIVE: Information that provides the reader with the principles that they are to apply to their lives.

DESCRIPTIVE: Incidental material that describes the way something was done but is not necessarily meant to encourage the reader in the same action.

GENESIS 2:24
"Therefore a man shall leave his father and his mother and hold fast to his wife, and they shall become one flesh."

QUESTIONS TO ASK YOURSELF ABOUT NARRATIVE:
Is there a command to be obeyed?
Is there a sin to avoid?
Is there an example to follow?
Is there a promise to claim?

NEWSPAPER ESCHATOLOGY:
The practice of interpreting the prophetic and apocalyptic portions of Scripture in light of current events.

ALLEGORICAL INTERPRETATION:
The process of interpreting the Scriptures as allegory, with every passage having a hidden symbolic layer of meaning.

2 TIM. 2:11-14

It is a trustworthy statement:
For if we died with Him, we shall also live with Him;
If we endure, we shall also reign with Him;
If we deny Him, He also will deny us;
If we are faithless, He remains faithful; for He cannot deny Himself."

THIRD COMMANDMENT
EX. 20:7

You shall not take the name of the Lord your God in vain, for the Lord will not leave him unpunished who takes His name in vain.

TIMELESS AUDIENCE

2. THEOLOGICAL STATEMENT

DEUT. 13
DEUT. 18
JER. 23

God's people are not to use His name in an attempt to gain power or give validity to their statements when He has not spoken.

ANALOGY OF SCRIPTURE

CONTEXTUALIZE PRINCIPLES FOR TODAY

TIME BOUND AUDIENCE

1. EXEGETICAL STATEMENT

God tells the Isrealites that they are not to use His name as the culture of the day used the names of their gods, using them to cast spells or pronounce blessings or curses.

ANCIENT AUDIENCE

3. HOMILETICAL STATEMENT

Don't use God's name, saying He said something He did not say.

CONTEMPORARY AUDIENCE

FIELD OPS:LITERARY GAP

ADDITIONAL TRAINING:
How to Read the Bible as Literature by Leland Ryken

GROUP DISCUSSION QUESTIONS:

1. Describe at least two different types of genre or literature you have engaged in today. What are the different rules that you applied to reading those genres? Did you have to pull out a "rule book" to remember these rules? Why or Why not?

2. How might the fact that Proverbs are not promises change your understanding?

3. Describe how we might commit the Incidental Fallacy.

4. How did this lesson challenge you most?

4. BRIDGING THE CONTEXTUAL GAP

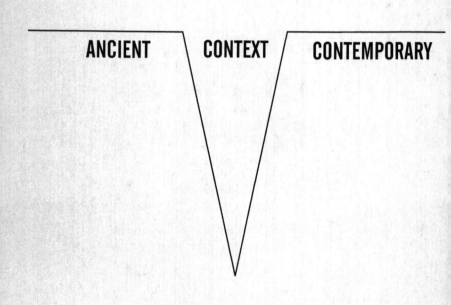

ANCIENT   CONTEXT   CONTEMPORARY

BASIC TRAINING:CONTEXT

You can make the Bible say whatever you want it to say so long as you ignore the context.

THE BIBLE SUPPORT ATHEISM:
PS. 53:1
"There is no God."

THE BIBLE SUPPORT SUICIDE:
MATT. 27:5
"He departed, and he went and hanged himself."

JUDG. 9:48
"What you have seen me do, hurry and do as I have done."

JOHN 13:27
"What you are going to do, do quickly."

THE BIBLE SUPPORTS CURSING GOD:
JOB 2:9

"Do you still hold fast your integrity? Curse God and die."

THE BIBLE SUPPORTS GETTING DRUNK:
GEN. 9:20-21

"Then Noah began farming and planted a vineyard. He drank of the wine and became drunk."

ECC. 3:1

"There is an appointed time for everything. And there is time for every event under heaven."

TYPES OF CONTEXT:

Context of the Argument

Context of Authorial Disposition

Context of Authorial Style

Context of Theological History

Context of Rhetoric

1. CONTEXT OF THE ARGUMENT:

Describes that which goes before and that which comes after the text you are studying, forming the "argument of the passage."

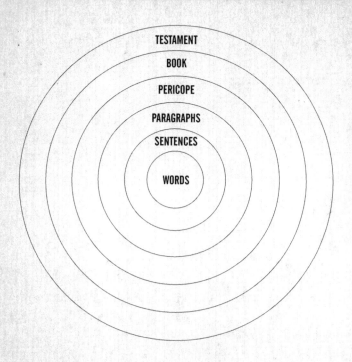

TESTAMENT

BOOK

PERICOPE

PARAGRAPHS

SENTENCES

WORDS

2. CONTEXT OF AUTHORIAL DISPOSITION:

Describes the attitude of the author when the work was composed which contributes to the tone.

WHAT WAS THE ATTITUDE OF THE AUTHOR WHEN HE WROTE?

Defensive? (2 Cor.)

Discouraged about life? (Eccl.)

Frustrated with the situation? (Jam.)

Baffled? (Gal.)

Proud of his audience? (Phil.)

Neural toward readers, passionate about subject? (Rom., Eph.)

3. CONTEXT OF AUTHORIAL STYLE:

Refers to the writing style and capabilities of the author.

John: simple writing style, extreme use of esoteric concepts (light, dark, word, love, hate)

Paul: logical, passionate, and excited writing style

James: pastoral and often sarcastic

David: passionate and emotional

Luke: detailed and historical

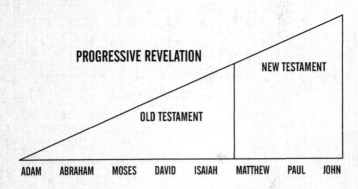

4. CONTEXT OF THEOLOGICAL HISTORY:
Refers to the time in history when the work was composed, understanding that there was a progressive unfolding of revelation throughout history.

Does the context limit the application?

Does new revelation limit or eliminate the application?

Does the passage apply to Israel or all people?

Is the practice in harmony with the rest of Scripture?

5. CONTEXT OF RHETORIC

Refers to how the author intended one to interpret his own words considering the rhetoric employed.

Is the author/speaker using hyperbole and exaggeration?

Is the author being sarcastic?

Is the author setting up a diatribe?

DO THESE PASSAGES APPLY TO THEOCRATIC ISRAEL OR THE CHURCH?

JOEL 2:25

"Then I will make up to you for the years that the swarming locust has eaten, the creeping locust, the stripping locust, and the gnawing locust, my great army which I sent among you."

JER. 29:11

"For I know the plans I have for you, declares the LORD, plans for welfare and not for evil, to give you a future and a hope."

2 CHRON. 7:14

"If my people who are called by my name humble themselves, and pray and seek my face and turn from their wicked ways, then I will hear from heaven and will forgive their sin and heal their land."

WHERE DOES THIS PASSAGE FIT IN THE CONTEXT OF THE STORY OR ARGUMENT?

ROM. 2:6-7

[God] will render to every man according to his deeds: to those who by perseverance in doing good seek for glory and honor and immortality, eternal life.

How do we know when to listen to an author and when not to?

Job's Friends?

Nebuchadnezzar?

King Solomon?

Peter before Pentecost?

Is this an exaggeration?

1 TIM. 6:3-4

"If anyone advocates a different doctrine and does not agree with sound words, those of our Lord Jesus Christ, and with the doctrine conforming to godliness, he is conceited and understands nothing"

COMBAT TRAINING:CONTEXT

OBSCURITY FALLACY:
Building theology from obscure material

READER RESPONSE FALLACY:
Reading passages out of context and applying them immediately to your situation by asking "What does this mean to me?"

FIELD OPS:CONTEXT

MATT. 18:20

"For where two or three are gathered in my name, there am I among them."

GROUP DISCUSSION QUESTIONS:

1. How do you think people have traditionally understood the above Bible passage?

2. Find the context of the passage in your Bible. Where does the section that this verse occurs begin? (Hint: read a few verses up)

3. Read the entire section.

4. What is the subject of this section (i.e. what is this section talking about)?

5. Considering the subject of this section, what does it mean to have 2 or 3 gathered in Christ's name in this context? (Hint: read verse 16 again).

6. How did this lesson challenge you most?

www.credohouse.org

Made in the USA
San Bernardino, CA
23 August 2018